RECORDED VERSIONS GUITAR ®

AUTHENTIC TRANSCRIPTIONS
WITH NOTES AND TABLATURE

dc Talk
SUPERNATURAL

Music transcriptions by Colin Higgins, Paul Pappas, and Jeffrey Story

Photography: covers, Alistair Thain; band, Len Peltier

ISBN 0-634-00085-3

HAL•LEONARD® CORPORATION

7777 W. BLUEMOUND RD. P.O. BOX 13819 MILWAUKEE, WI 53213

Visit Hal Leonard Online at
www.halleonard.com

dc Talk
SUPERNATURAL

CONTENTS

It's Killing Me

Words and Music by Toby McKeehan, Michael Tait, Kevin Max and Greg Wells

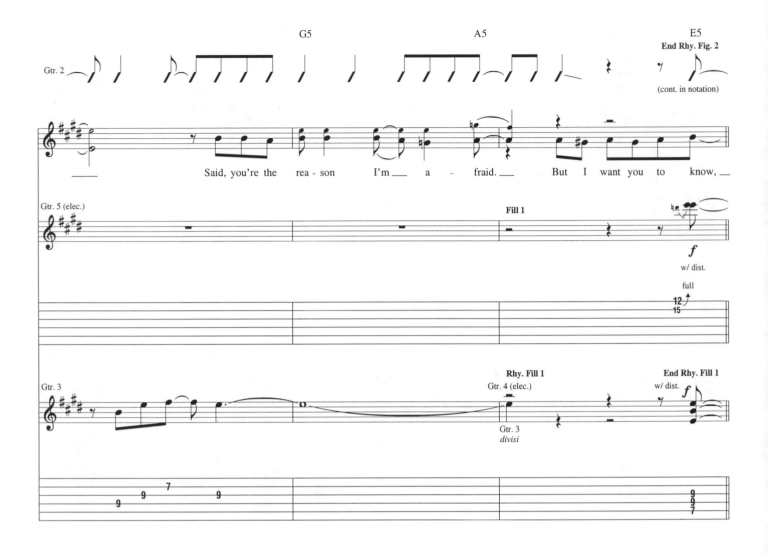

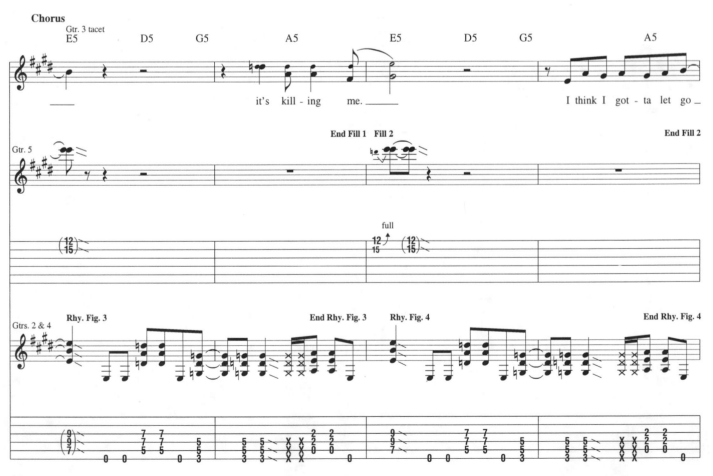

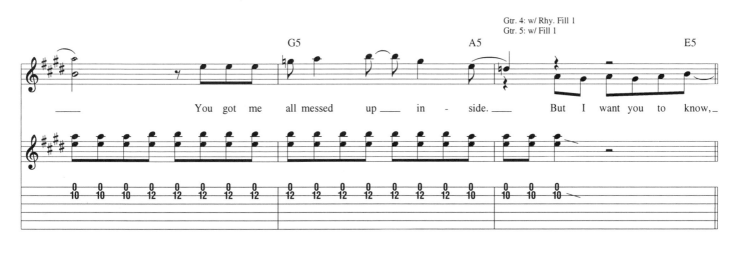

You got me all messed up ___ in - side. ___ But I want you to know, ___

Chorus

it's kill - ing me. ___ I think I got - ta let go ___

'cause it's kill - ing me. ___ And I want you to know, ___

(Kill - ing me. ___) it's kill - ing me. ___ I think I need to let go ___

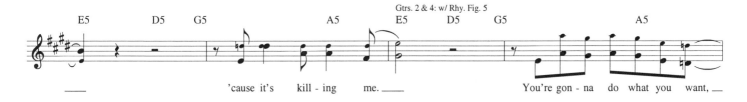

'cause it's kill - ing me. ___ You're gon - na do what you want, ___

but you bet - ter be - lieve. ___ Is it

(cont. in slash)

Chorus

Bkgd. Voc.: w/ Voc. Fig. 2, 8 times
Gtrs. 2 & 4: w/ Rhy. Fig. 3
Gtrs. 2 & 4: w/ Rhy. Fig. 4, 7 times, simile
Gtr. 5: w/ Fill 2, 7 times

it's kill-ing me. ___ I think I got-ta let go ___

(And I got-ta let go. ___) 'cause it's kill-ing me. ___ It's kill-ing me. ___ And I want you to know, ___

And I want you to know, ___ it's kill-ing me. ___ it's kill-ing me. ___ I think I need to let go ___

And I need to let go. ___ 'cause it's kill-ing me. ___ It's kill-ing me. ___ It's kill-ing me. ___) It's kill-ing me. ___

Outro

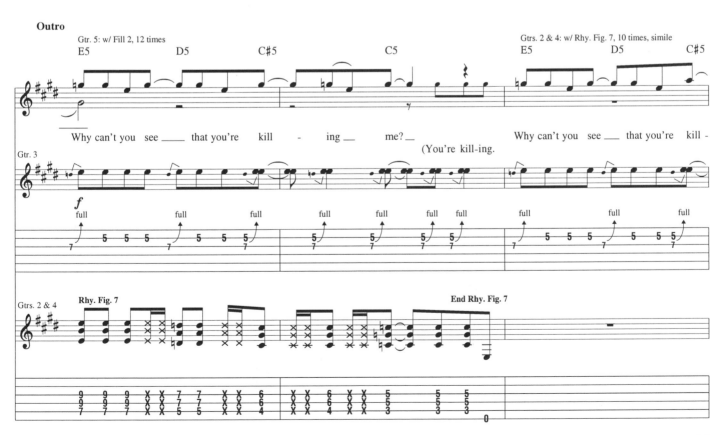

Why can't you see ___ that you're kill - ing ___ me? ___ (You're kill-ing.

Why can't you see ___ that you're kill -

Gtr. 3

Gtrs. 2 & 4

Rhy. Fig. 7

End Rhy. Fig. 7

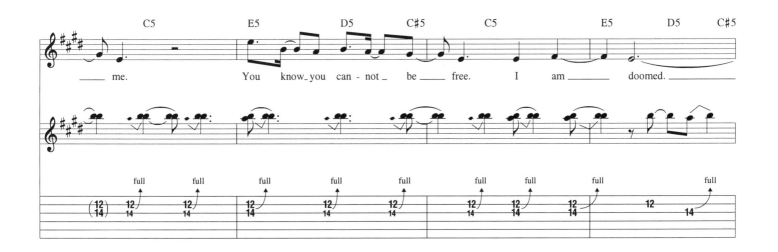

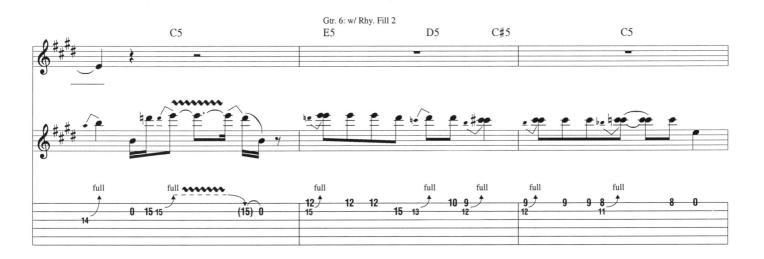

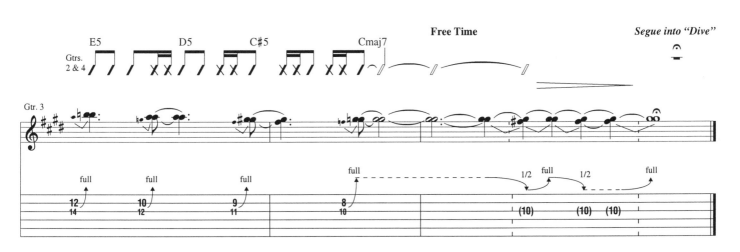

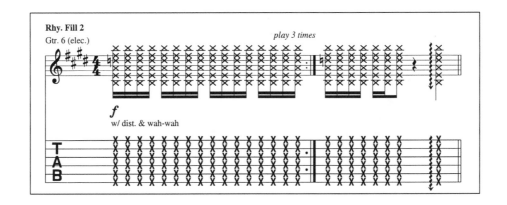

Dive

Words and Music by Toby McKeehan, Michael Tait, Kevin Max and Mark Heimermann

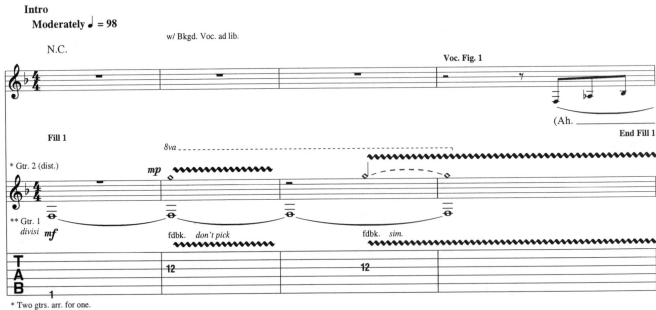

* Two gtrs. arr. for one.

** Synth. arr for gtr. Segued from previous track.

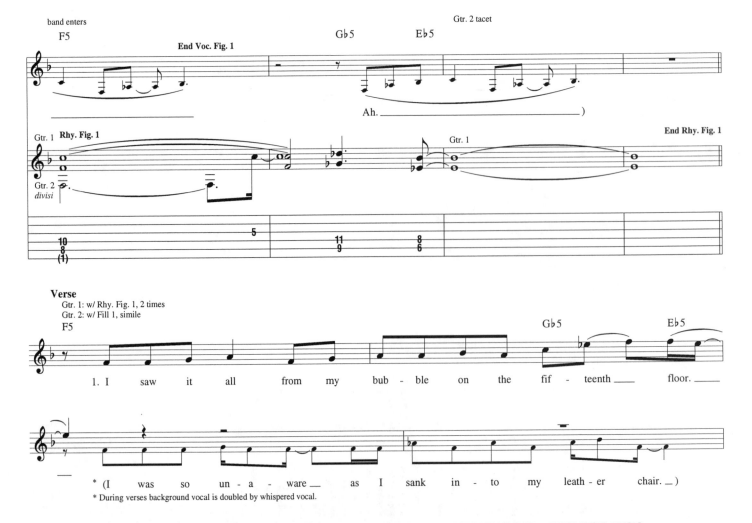

* During verses background vocal is doubled by whispered vocal.

this would shape my des - ti - ny. __)

Take my hand, un - der - stand you are not a - lone. __

*(Take my hand, un - der - stand you are not a - lone. __
* not doubled

Oh, __ the stir - ring of __ the Ho - ly Ghost. __
__)

(Shame on me if I op - pose __ the stir - ring of the Ho - ly Ghost. __)

Pre-Chorus
Gtr. 2: w/ Rhy. Fig. 2

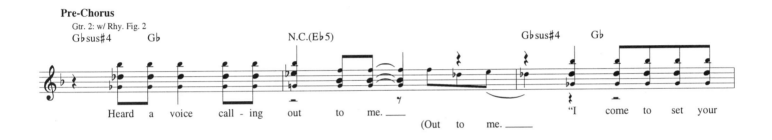

Heard a voice call - ing out to me. __

(Out to me. __

"I come to set your

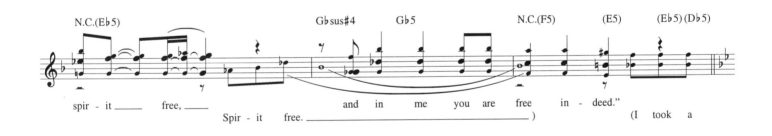

spir - it __ free, __

Spir - it free. __

and in me you are free in - deed."

)

(I took a

𝄋 **Chorus**
Bkgd. Voc.: w/ Voc. Fig. 2
Gtr. 2: w/ Rhy. Fig. 3, 2 times

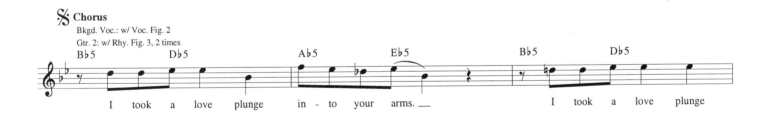

I took a love plunge in - to your arms. __

I took a love plunge

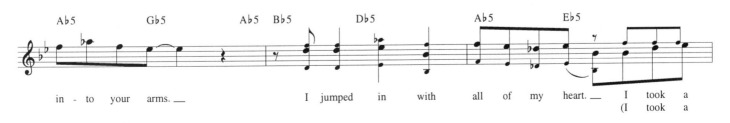

in - to your arms. __

I jumped in with all of my heart. __

I took a
(I took a

Consume Me

Words and Music by Toby McKeehan, Michael Tait, Kevin Max and Mark Heimermann

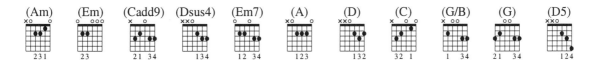

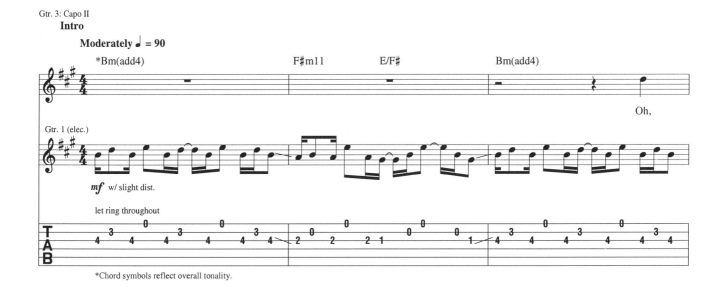

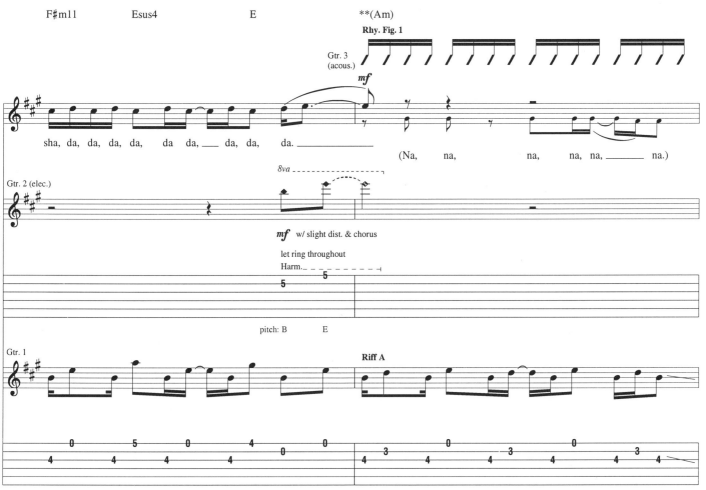

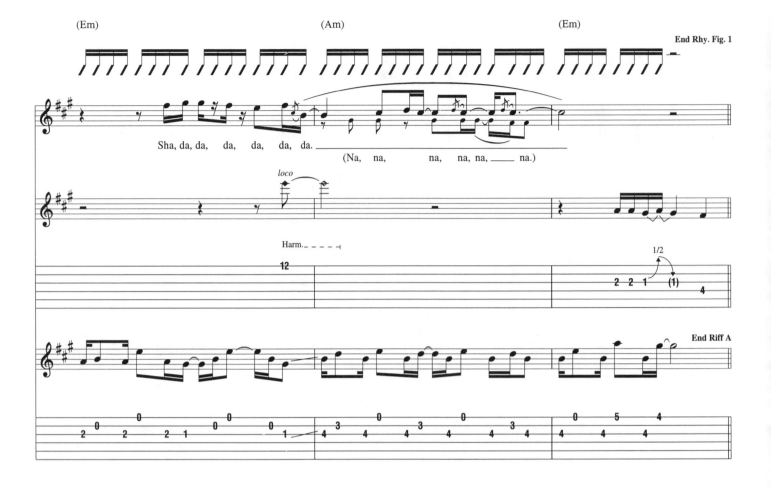

Sha, da, da, da, da, da, da.
(Na, na, na, na, na, na.)

Verse

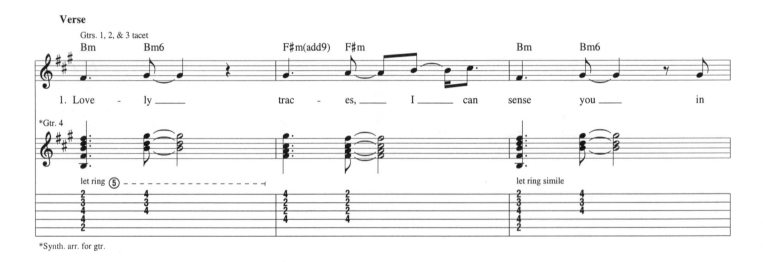

1. Love - ly trac - es, I can sense you in ev - 'ry - thing.

*Synth. arr. for gtr.

ev - 'ry - thing. The way that you move me takes me

Gtr. 4 tacet

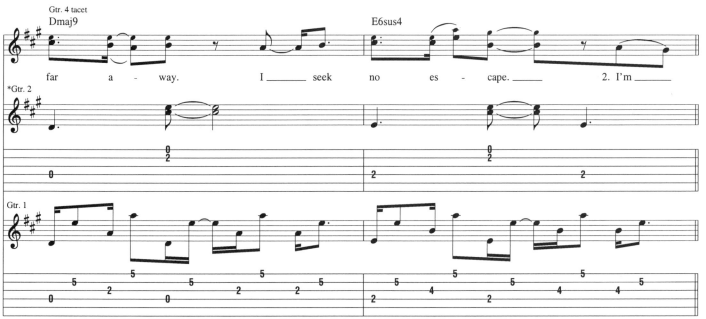

*Increase depth setting on chorus to simulate vibrato effect.

Verse

27

Chorus

Pre-Chorus

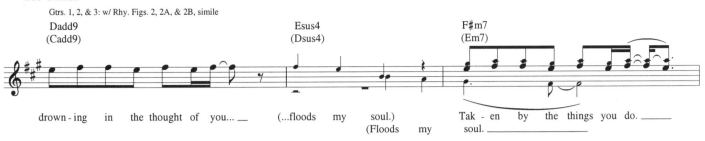

drown-ing in the thought of you... _ (...floods my soul.) Tak- en by the things you do. _____
(Floods my soul. _____

(God, you know it...) ...does- n't mat- ter what I lose. _ I'm yours. ____ You con- sume _
God, you know. _____)

Chorus

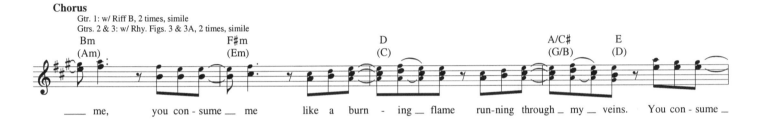

____ me, you con- sume _ me like a burn- ing _ flame run-ning through _ my _ veins. You con- sume _

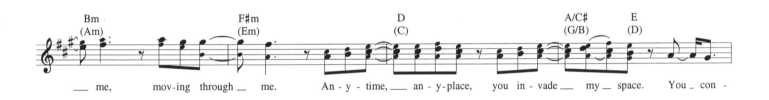

____ me, mov-ing through _ me. An- y- time, _ an- y-place, you in- vade _ my _ space. You _ con-

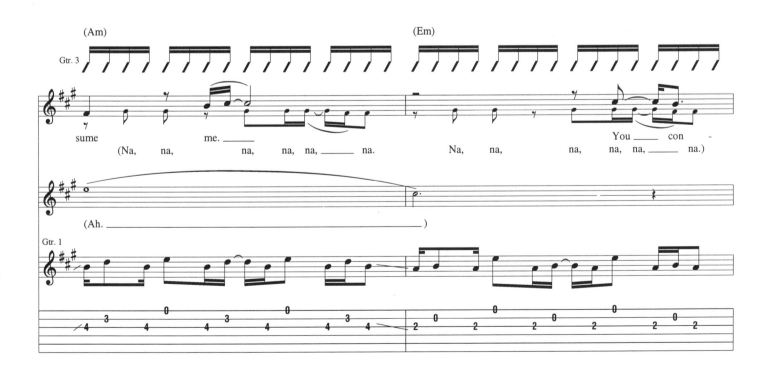

sume me. _ You ____ con-
(Na, na, na, na, na, _____ na. Na, na, na, na, na, _____ na.)

(Ah. _____)

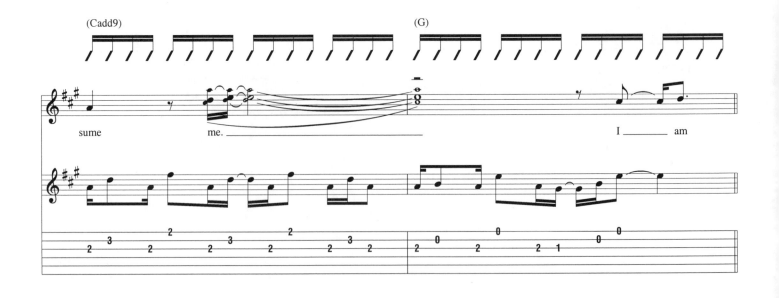

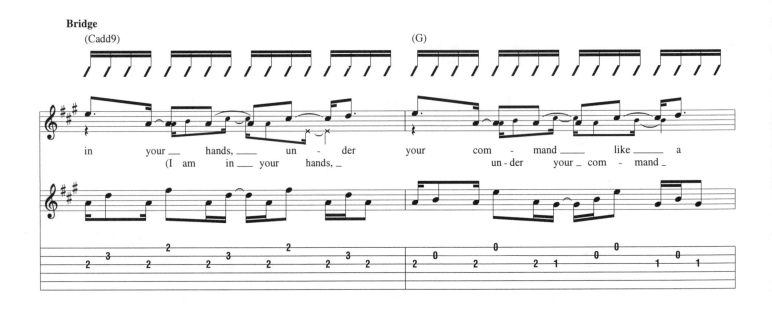

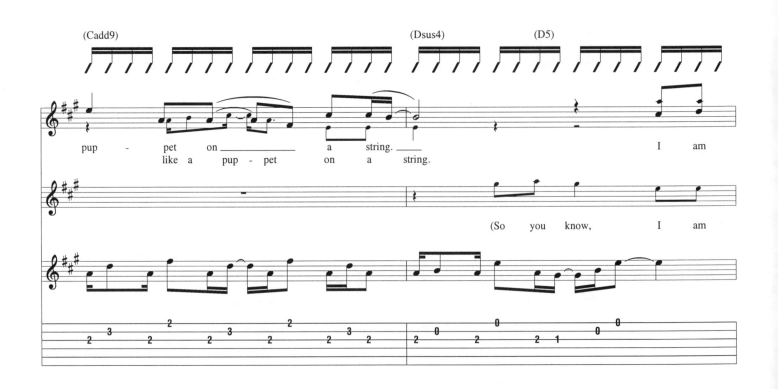

My Friend (So Long)

Words and Music by Toby McKeehan, Michael Tait, Kevin Max, Mark Hudson and Dominick Miller

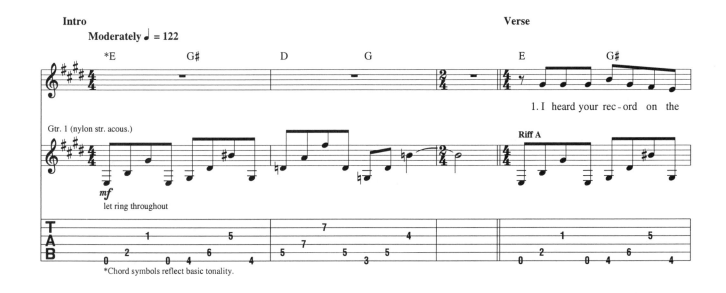

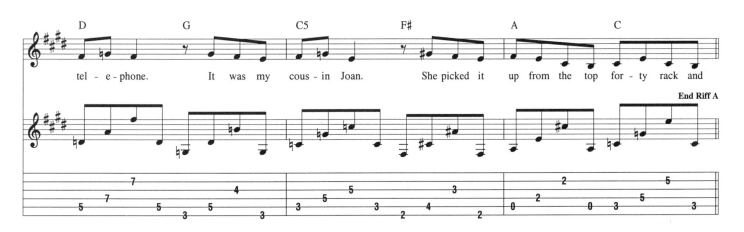

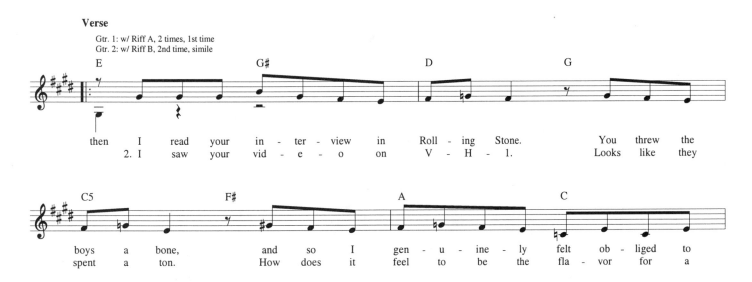

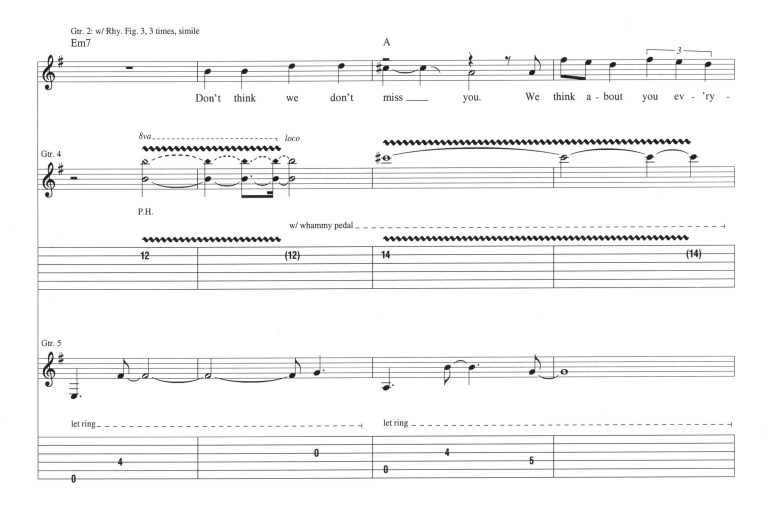

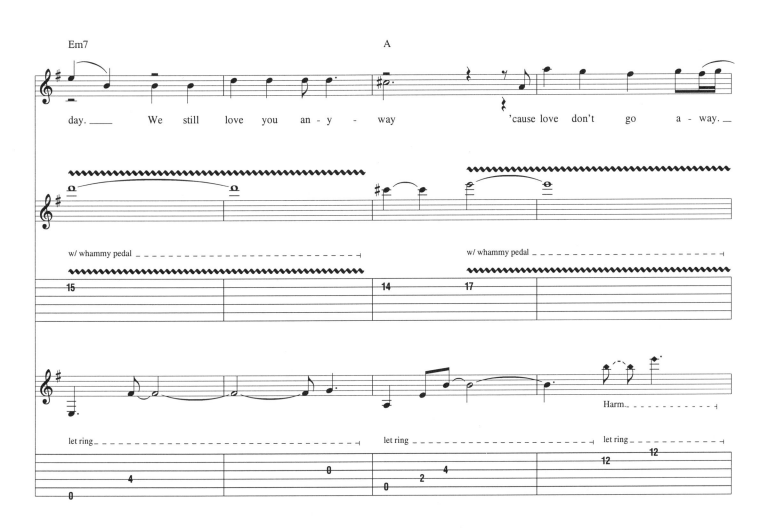

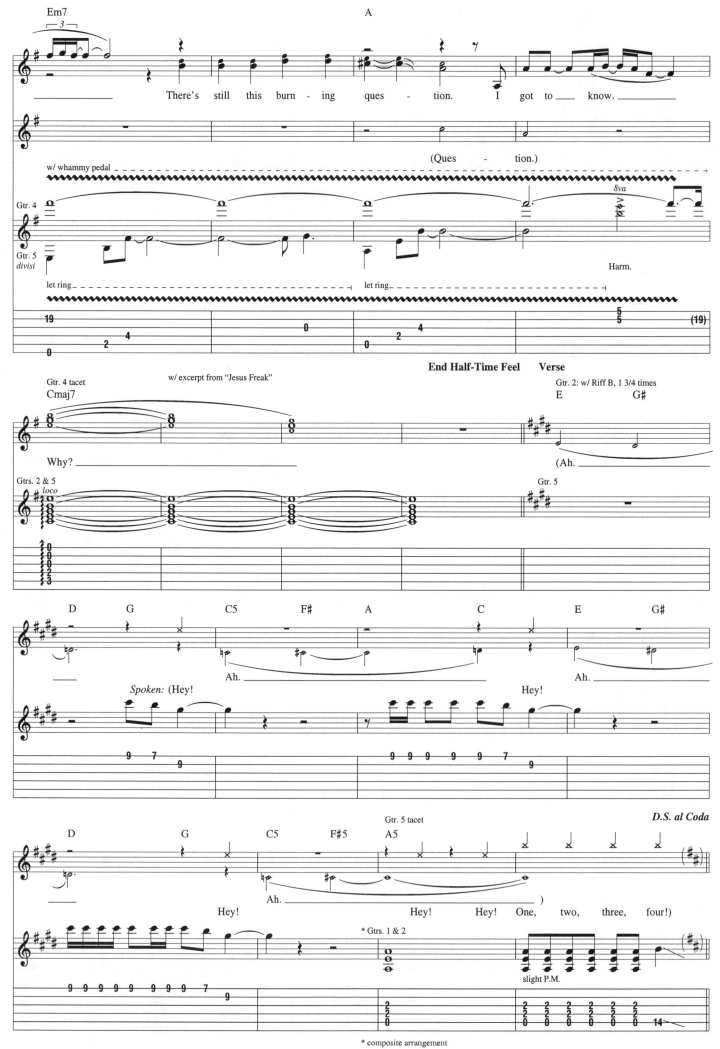

Fearless

Words and Music by Toby McKeehan, Michael Tait, Kevin Max, Mark Heimermann and George Cocchini

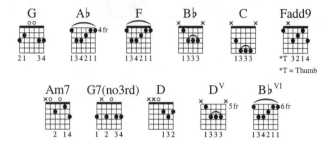

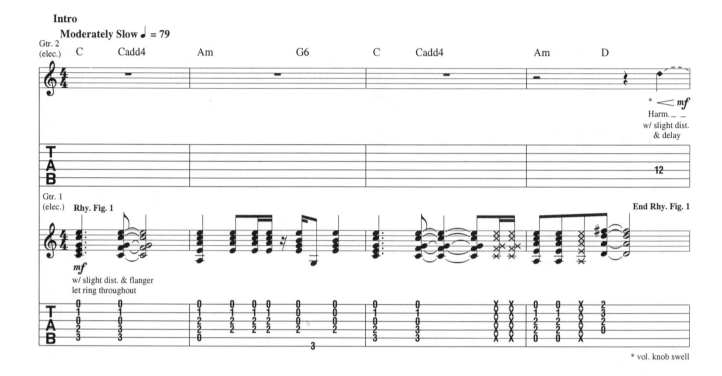

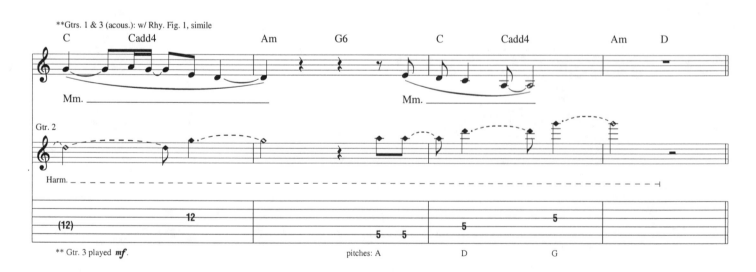

1. Haunt - ed by ___ a jad - ed past, ___ nev - er thought ___ that love ___ could last. ___

Turned me a-round and ya got me be-liev-in' you would die for me. Now I'm
(Turned me a-round.)

Chorus

fear - less _____ with noth-ing left to hide. _ All the doubts_
(Fear - less,

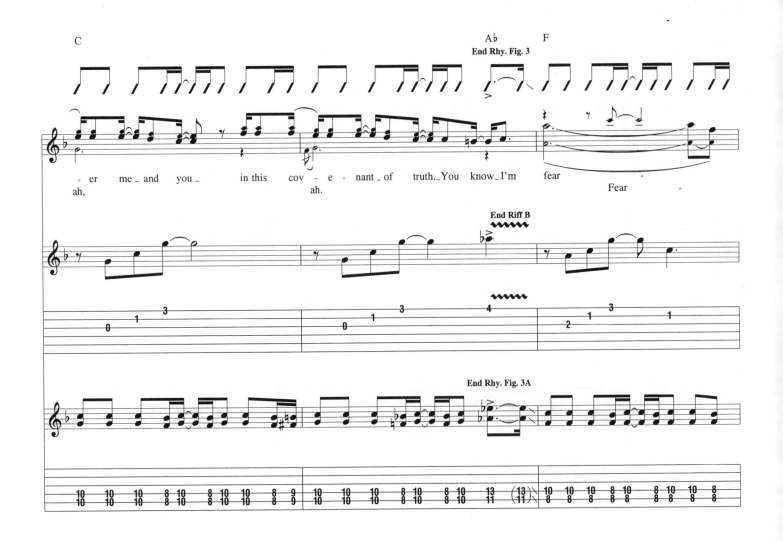

Verse

Gtrs. 1 & 3: w/ Rhy. Fig. 1, 2 times, simile
Gtrs. 2 & 6 tacet

2. Pa - tient - ly ___ you stripped ___ a - way ___ the walls of pride ___ that I ___ had raised. ___

You re - vealed ___ the child ___ in - side of me. _____ Yeah, ___ we will run ___ and not ___ grow old, _____

Gtr. 2

soar on wings ___ as I've ___ been told. To - geth - er we ___ will fly _____ the heav - en - lies. ___ 'Cause
(As I've been told.)

pitch: G
* vol. swell

Pre-Chorus

Gtrs. 1, 3, & 4: w/ Rhy. Fig. 2
Gtr. 2: w/ Riff A, simile

Fadd9   Am7

out of the noise I could hear you breath - ing. You came a - long know - ing just what I need - ed.
(Out of the noise.)   You came a - long.

Gtr. 6

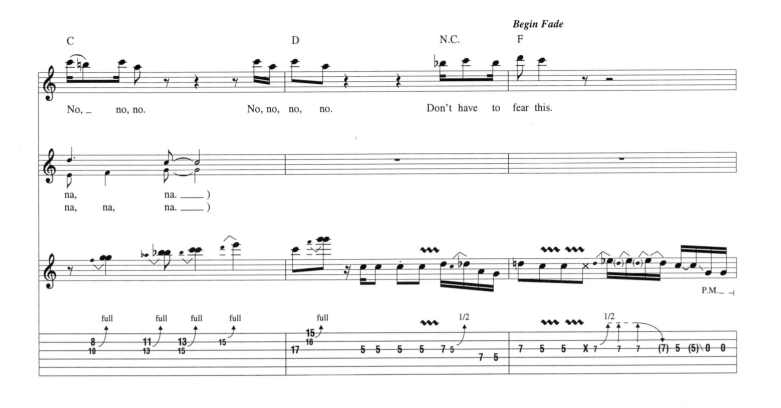

No, _ no, no. No, no, no, no. Don't have to fear this.

na,   na,   na. _____)
na, na,   na. _____)

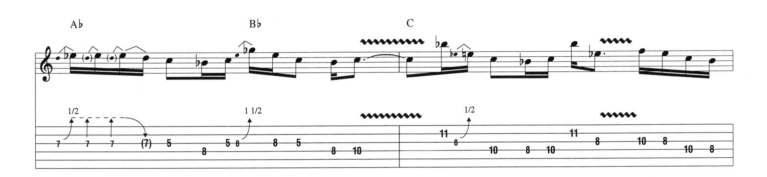

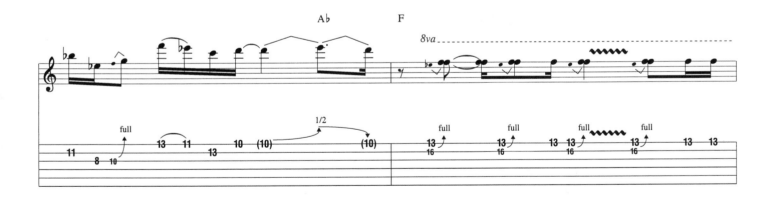

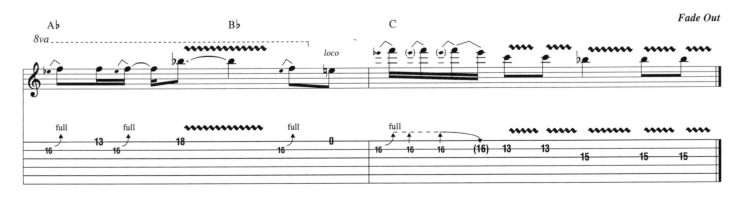

Godsend

Words and Music by Toby McKeehan, Michael Tait, Kevin Max, Mark Heimermann and Chad Chapin

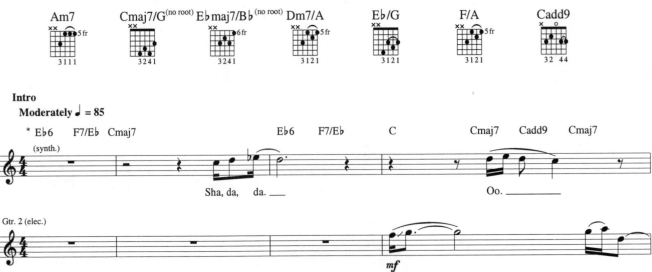

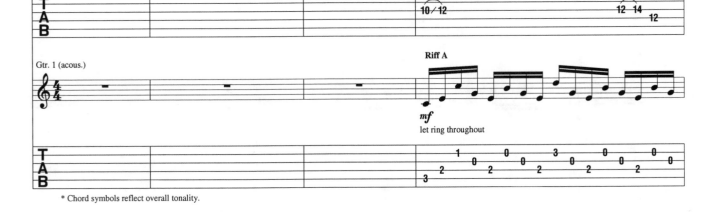

* Chord symbols reflect overall tonality.

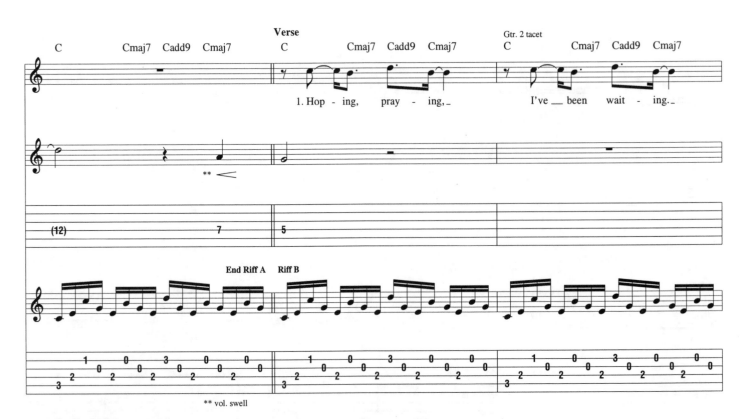

** vol. swell

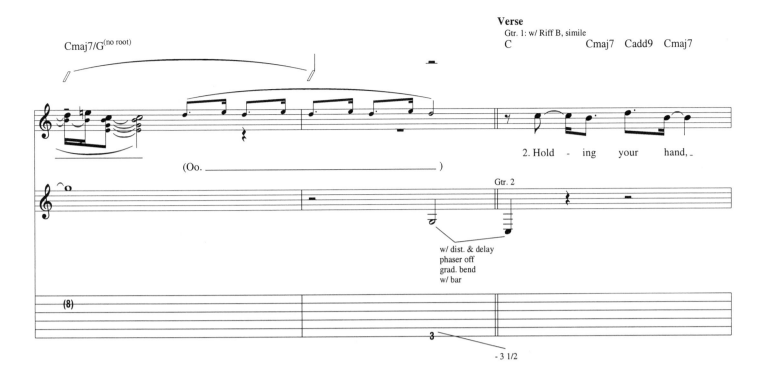

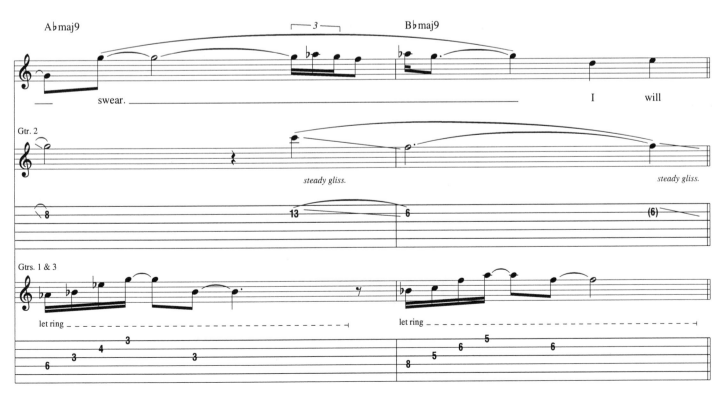

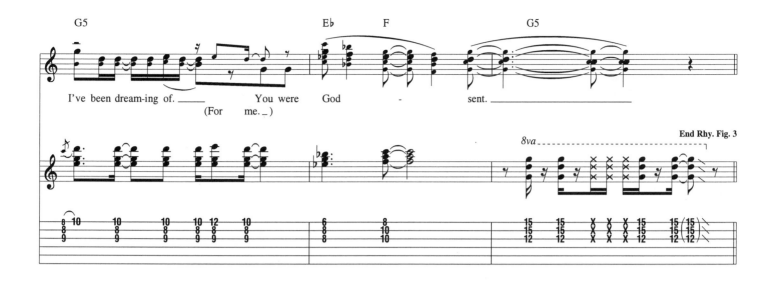

I've been dream-ing of. _____ You were God - sent. _____
(For me. _)

Bridge
Gtr. 4 tacet

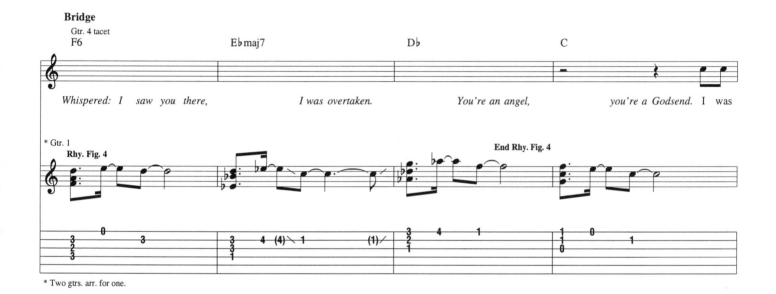

Whispered: I saw you there, I was overtaken. You're an angel, you're a Godsend. I was

*Two gtrs. arr. for one.

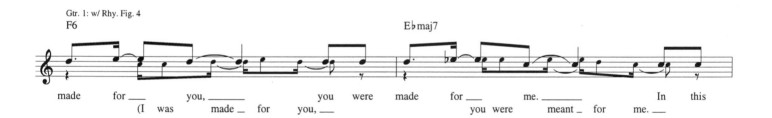

made for _____ you, _____ you were made for _____ me. _____ In this
(I was made _ for you, _____ you were meant _ for me. _)

lone-ly _____ world, _____ we were meant to _____ be _____ in love. I will
In this lone-ly world _____ we were meant _ to be _ in love.)

63

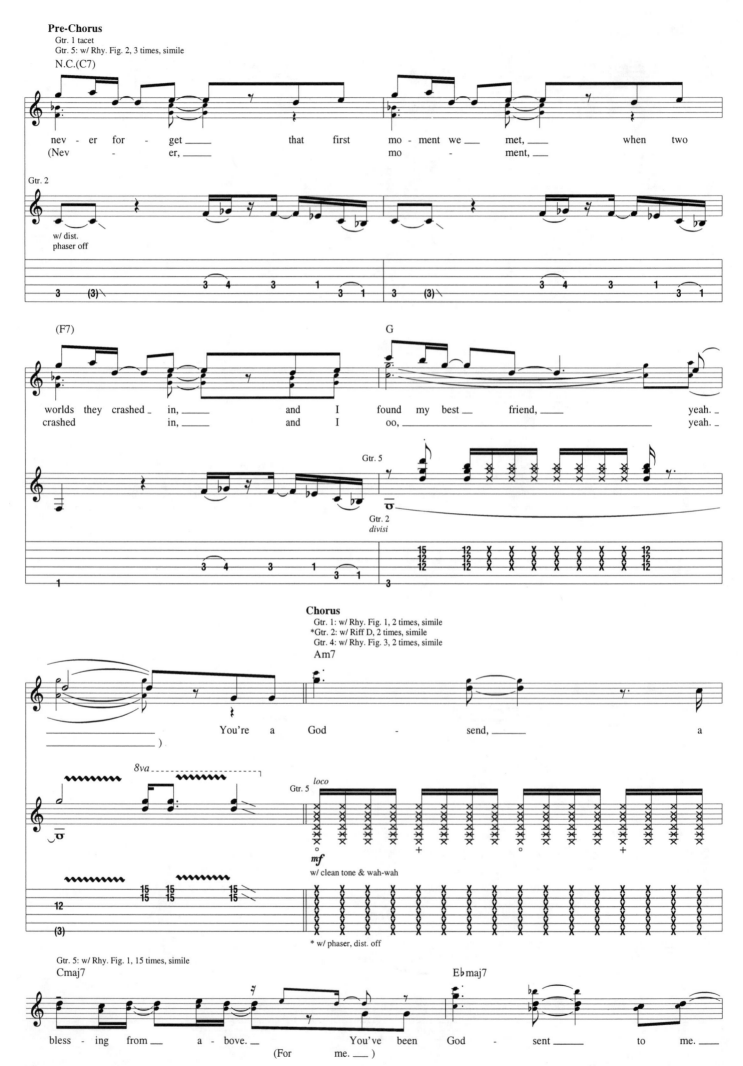

You're a God - send, — I've been dream-ing of. — You're a
(We were meant — to be. —) (For me. —)

God - send. — You're a God - send, — an
Oh, — yeah, ah, — yeah. Oh, — woah.

an - gel from — a-bove. — You've been God - sent — to me. — We were meant — to be. —
(For me. —)
Send an an - gel. Oh, you know it's true. — Dar - ling you're a...

God - send, — I've been dream-ing of. — You were God - sent. —
For me. —)
God sent an an - gel, God sent an an - gel to — me. Oh,

Gtr. 1: w/ Rhy. Fig. 1, last 2 meas., simile
Gtr. 2: w/ Riff D, last 2 meas., simile
Gtr. 4: w/ Rhy. Fig. 3, last 2 meas., simile

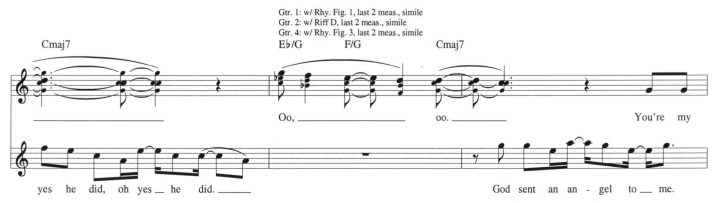

— Oo, — oo. — You're my
yes he did, oh yes — he did. — God sent an an - gel to — me.

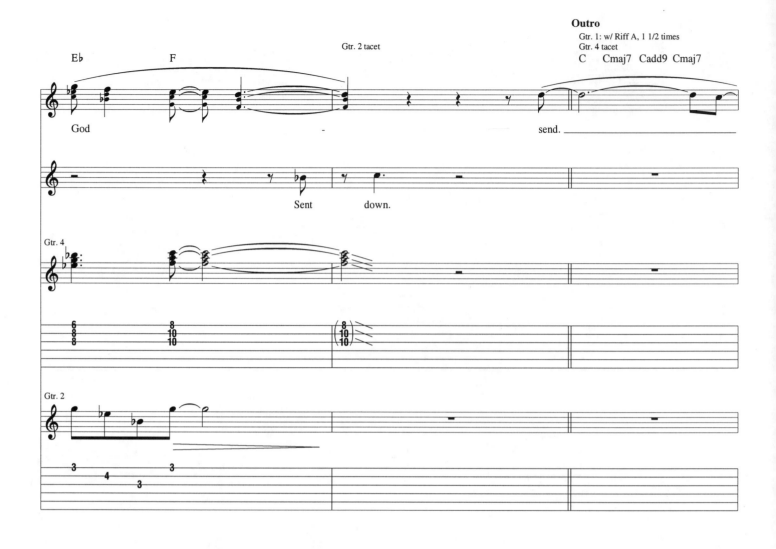

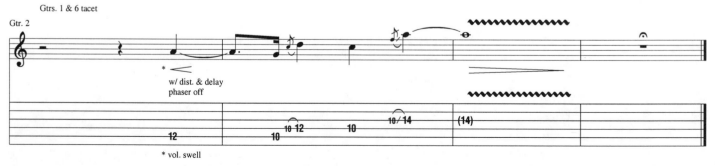

Wanna Be Loved

Words and Music by Toby McKeehan, Michael Tait, Kevin Max and Mark Heimermann

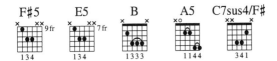

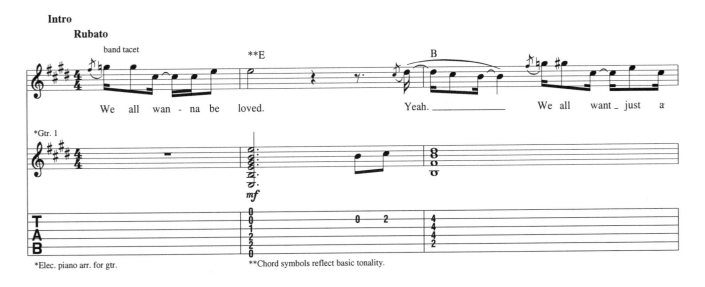

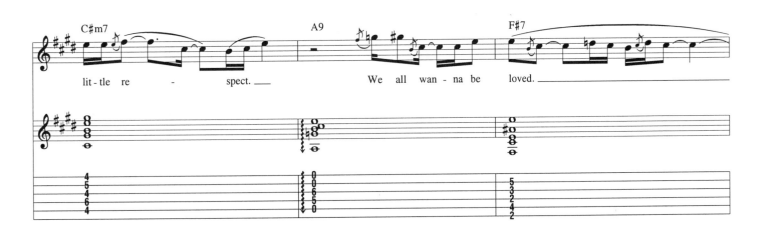

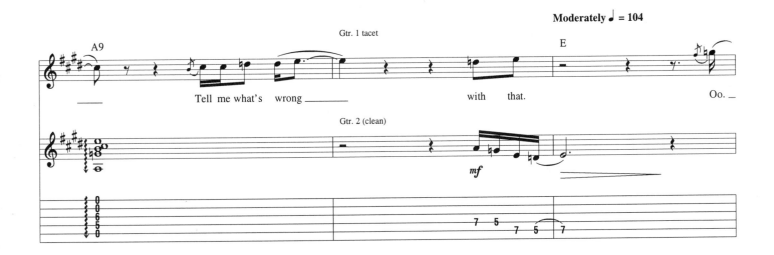

sep - 'rate __ worlds. __   But one thing that we've got in com - mon __ is we all wan - na be

Sep - 'rate worlds. __)

End Rhy. Fig. 2

Chorus

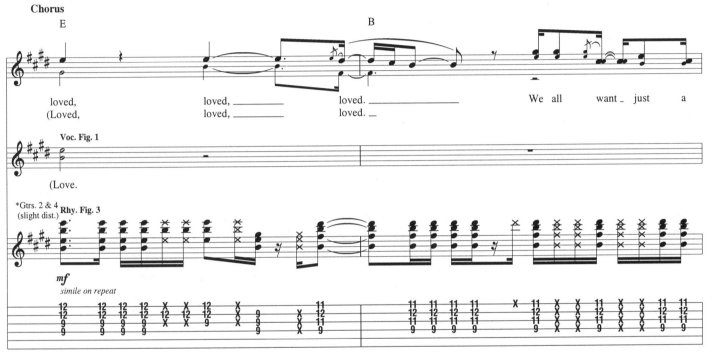

loved,   loved, _____ loved. _____   We all want __ just a

(Loved,   loved, _____ loved. __

Voc. Fig. 1

(Love.

*Gtrs. 2 & 4
(slight dist.) **Rhy. Fig. 3**

mf
simile on repeat

* composite arrangement

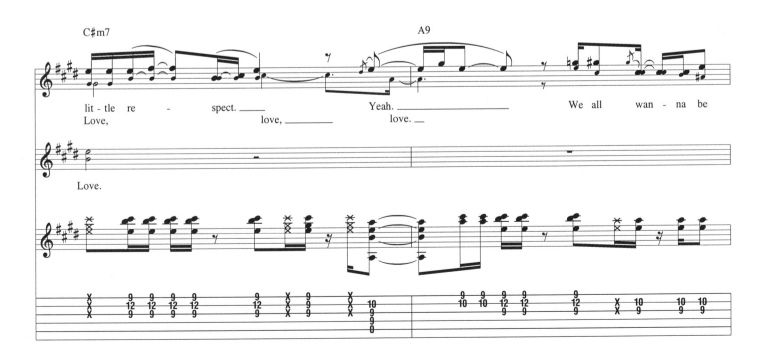

lit - tle re - spect. _____   Yeah. _____   We all wan - na be

Love,   love, _____   love. __

Love.

We all wan - na be loved. _____ Oo, tell me what's wrong with that. __
Love, love, __ love. Tell me what's wrong with that. __

Gtr. 2: w/ Rhy. Fig. 4, simile

Bkgd. Voc.: w/ Voc. Fig. 1, simile
Gtrs. 2 & 4: w/ Rhy. Fig. 3, 1st 5 meas. simile

__ yeah. Oh, _____ yeah. We all wan - na be loved, loved, __ loved. __
__ y'all.) (Loved, loved, __ loved. __

(We all wan - na be __ loved.)

We all want __ just a __ lit - tle _____ re - spect. _____
Love, love, _____ love. __

A, we all wan - na be loved. _____
Love, love, _____ love. __

Interlude
Gtr. 4 tacet

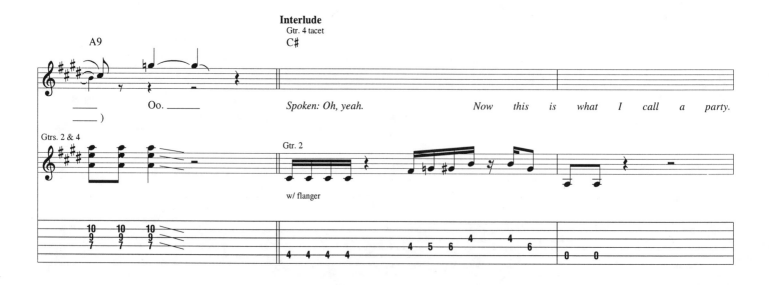

___ Oo. __ *Spoken: Oh, yeah.* *Now this is what I call a party.*
__)

Gtrs. 2 & 4

Gtr. 2

w/ flanger

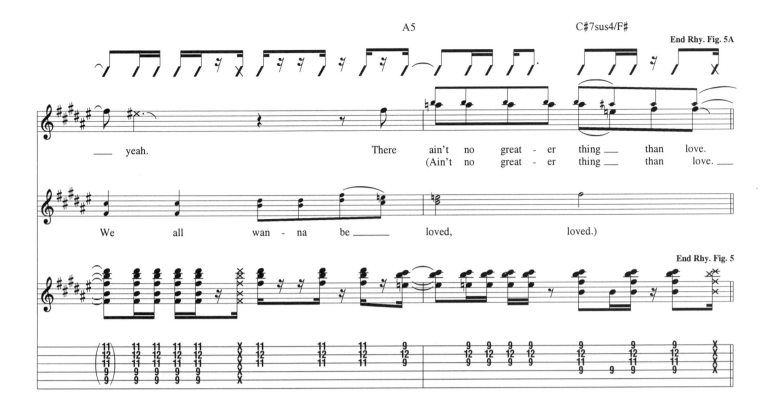

A5   C#7sus4/F#   End Rhy. Fig. 5A

___ yeah.   There ain't no great - er thing ___ than love.

(Ain't no great - er thing ___ than love. ___

We all wan - na be ___ loved,   loved.)

End Rhy. Fig. 5

Bkgd. Voc.: w/ Voc. Fig. 2, 4 times, simile
Lead Voc.: w/ Voc. ad lib., 2nd time
Gtrs. 2 & 4: w/ Rhy. Figs. 5 & 5A, 5 3/4 times, simile

F#5   E5   B   A5

_____ Whoa, _____ whoa. _____) It's the gift ___

2nd time, Begin Fade

C#7sus4/F# F#5   E5   B

ev - 'ry - bod - y knows. ___ Love is a thing that we __ all crave, _ and let us pray. __

A5   C#7sus4/F# F#5   E5

Love is a thing that we __ all crave, _ and let us pray. ___ Let us pray. ___ Love is a thing that we __ all crave, _ and

2nd time, Fade Out |1. |2.

B   A5   C#7sus4/F#   (synth.)

let us pray. _ Love is a thing that we __ all crave, _ and let us pray. _ Let us pray. _

The Truth

Words and Music by Toby McKeehan, Michael Tait, Kevin Max and Mark Heimermann

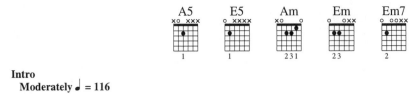

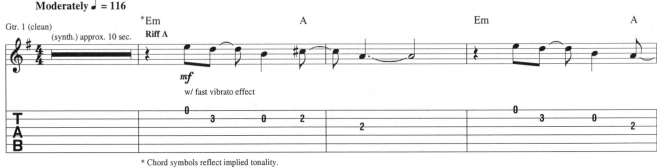

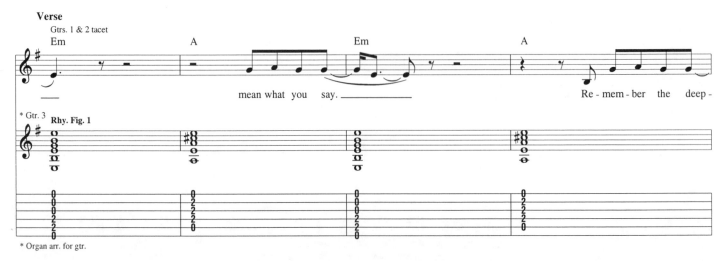

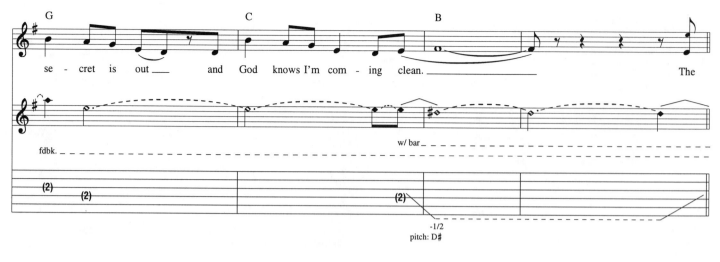

se- cret is out ___ and God knows I'm com - ing clean. ___ The

Chorus

truth ___ is what we need. It is the end of mys - ter - y. ___ The

D.S. al Coda 2

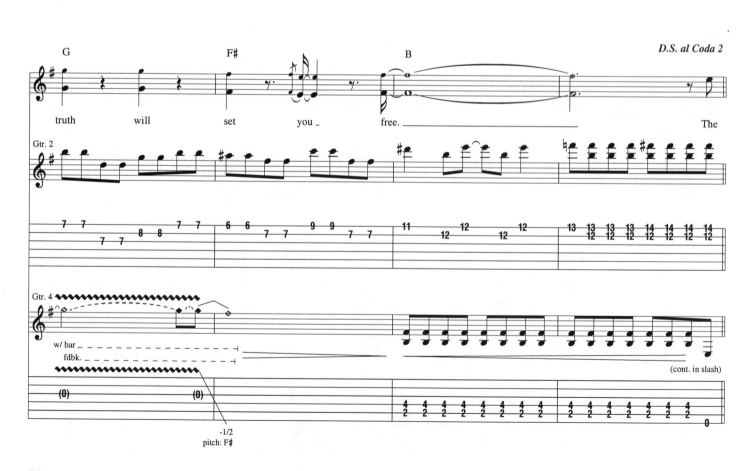

truth ___ will ___ set ___ you ___ free. ___ The

Since I Met You

Words and Music by Toby McKeehan, Michael Tait, Kevin Max and Mark Heimermann

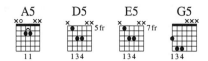

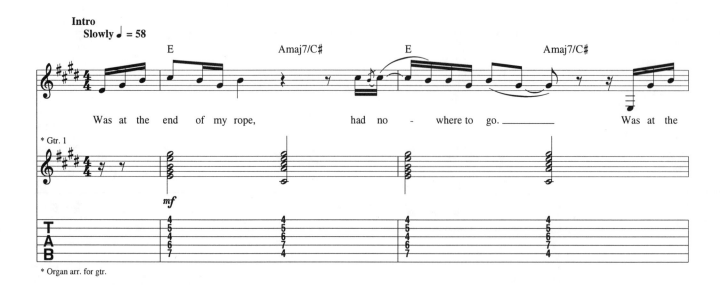

Was at the end of my rope, had no - where to go. _____ Was at the

* Organ arr. for gtr.

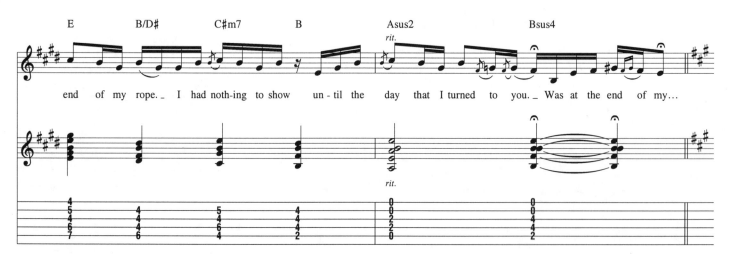

end of my rope. _ I had noth-ing to show un-til the day that I turned to you. _ Was at the end of my...

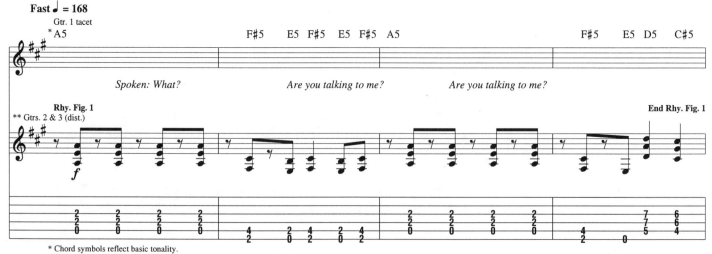

Spoken: What?   *Are you talking to me?*   *Are you talking to me?*

* Chord symbols reflect basic tonality.

** doubled throughout

Gtrs. 2 & 3: w/ Rhy. Fig. 1, simile

A5 | F#5 E5 F#5 | E5 F#5 A5 | F#5 E5 D5 C#5

Did you call me crazy?   *Did you call me crazy?!*   *Did you call me crazy?!!*   *Did you call me crazy?!!*

Verse

Gtr. 4: w/ Fill 1, 2nd time

A5   D5   A5   D5

1. Call me cra-zy, man, you make my __ day. __   My state of res-i-dence was dis-ar - ray. __
2. You got me feel-ing like a mil-lion __ bucks. __   Some peo-ple write it off as I - rish __ luck.

Gtrs. 2 & 3   **Rhy. Fig. 2**

P.M.

simile on repeat   *sim.*   (cont. in slash)

A5   A D5   E5   G5

⑤ open   **End Rhy. Fig. 2**

Gtrs. 2 & 3   P.M.

At ev-'ry par-ty and as far as an-y-bod-y knew _____ ev-'ry-thing was __ cool. But,
But I knew bet-ter 'cause my rab-bit's __ foot __ nev-er did _____ me a bit of __ good.

Gtr. 4 (dist.)

mf

let ring

Fill 1
Gtr. 4

Then love came knock - ing at my door.)
You made some - thing of my life.)
No, no, no.)

Since I met

Chorus
Bkgd. Voc.: w/ Voc. Fig. 1, 2nd and 3rd times
Gtrs. 4 & 5 tacet

you I've been al - right. ___ You turn all my dark - ness in - to light. ___

* Gtrs. 2 & 3
P.M. ___ P.M. ___ P.M. ___
simile on repeats

* composite arrangement

Voc. Fig. 1

(Since I ___ met you. Dark in - to ___ light. Since I ___ met you.

I've been ___ o - kay. Win - ter ___ to May. ___ Since I'm ___ al - right. ___

* Delay set for eighth-note triplet regeneration with 5 repeats.

No-where to go.

* Played ahead of the beat.

Into Jesus

Words and Music by Toby McKeehan, Michael Tait, Kevin Max and Mark Heimermann

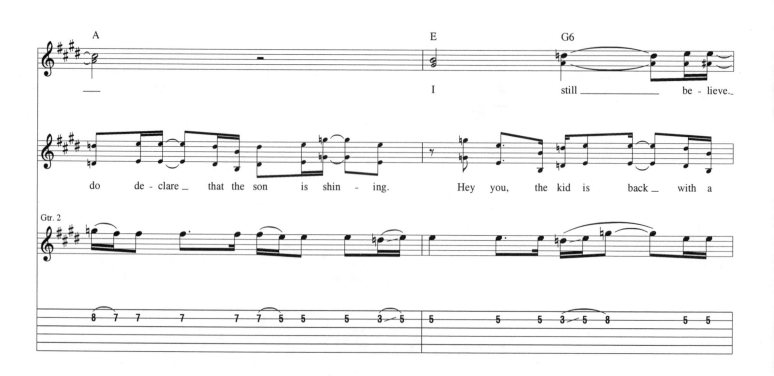

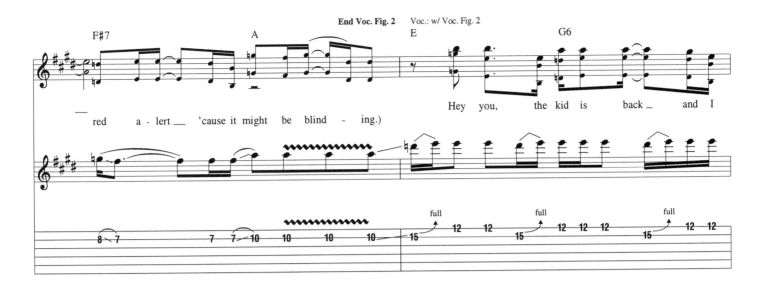

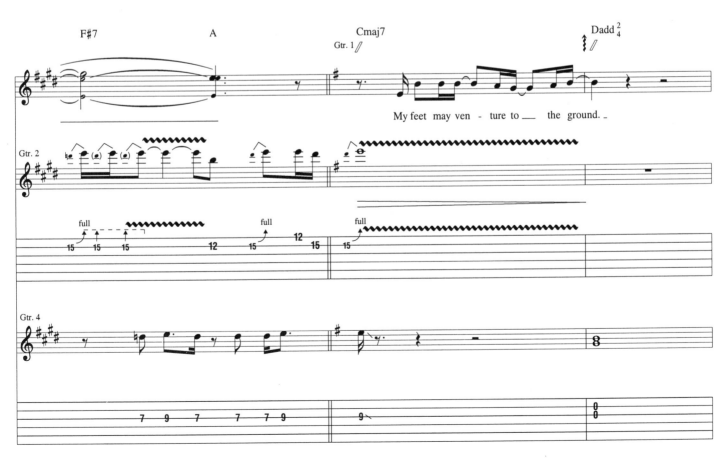

* vol. swells

**Gtr. 4 to left of slash in TAB.

you,   I've seen the truth. _____   Oo, _____ and I be - lieve. __

(Truth.)

Gtr. 2

Gtr. 4

Chorus

Voc.: w/ Voc. Fig. 1, 1st 6 meas.
Gtr. 1: w/ Rhy. Fig. 1, 7 times, simile
Gtrs. 2 & 3: w/ Riffs B & B1, 3 1/2 times, simile
Gtr. 4: w/ Riff C, 3 1/2 times

Em   C   G   D5   Em   C   G   D5

_____ Oh, __ ho.   I still be - lieve. _____ Whoa. ___   I'm in - to Je -

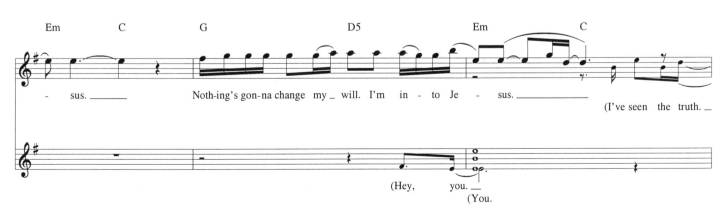

Em   C   G   D5   Em   C

- sus. _____   Noth-ing's gon-na change my _ will. I'm in - to Je - sus. _____

(I've seen the truth. _

(Hey,   you. (You.

Supernatural

Words and Music by Toby McKeehan, Michael Tait, Kevin Max and Mark Heimermann

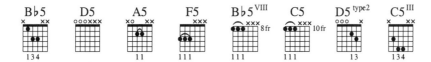

Drop D Tuning:
① = E ④ = D
② = B ⑤ = A
③ = G ⑥ = D

* Written one octave lower than actual pitch throughout.

Bridge

I need an in-ter-ven-tion. A touch of prov-i-dence. ___

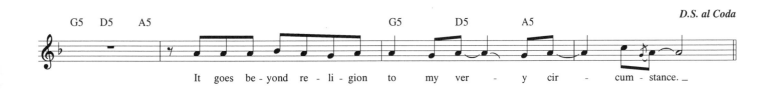

D.S. al Coda

It goes be-yond re-li-gion to my ver-y cir-cum-stance. ___

Coda

God is there ___ and He ___ is watch-ing. The signs are ev-'ry-where. ___ Oh, ___

Spoken: (The signs are ev-'ry-where.)

Voc. Fig. 2

(God _____ is ev-'ry-where. _

God is there. ___ There's no ___ de-ny-ing it's su-per-nat-u-ral. ___

Spoken: (It's su-per-nat-u-ral.)

End Voc. Fig. 2

God. _____ Yeah. _____)

Interlude
Half-Time Feel

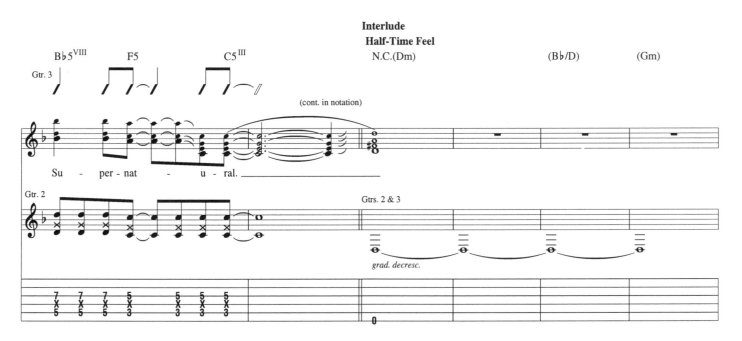

Su-per-nat-u-ral. _____

Gtrs. 2 & 3 tacet

Six days, a u - ni - verse ___ was made. ___

From the dead ___ a man ___ was raised. ___

Voc. Fig. 3   End Voc. Fig. 3

(Su - per - nat - u - ral. ___)

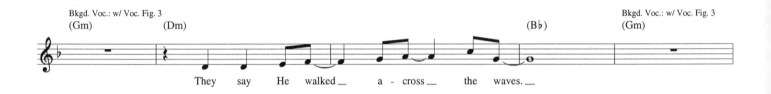

Bkgd. Voc.: w/ Voc. Fig. 3   Bkgd. Voc.: w/ Voc. Fig. 3

They say He walked ___ a - cross ___ the waves. ___

And I'll be - lieve ___ it to my grave. ___

Bridge

N.C.(D5)
(tape effects)

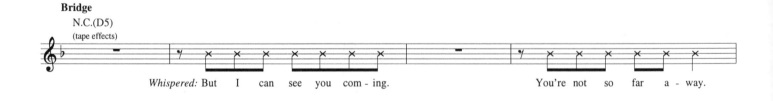

Whispered: But I can see you com - ing.   You're not so far a - way.

G5   D5   A5   G5   D5   A5

'Cause I can feel Your pow - er   Surg - ing through ___ the whole

Gtrs. 2 & 3

(cont. in slash)

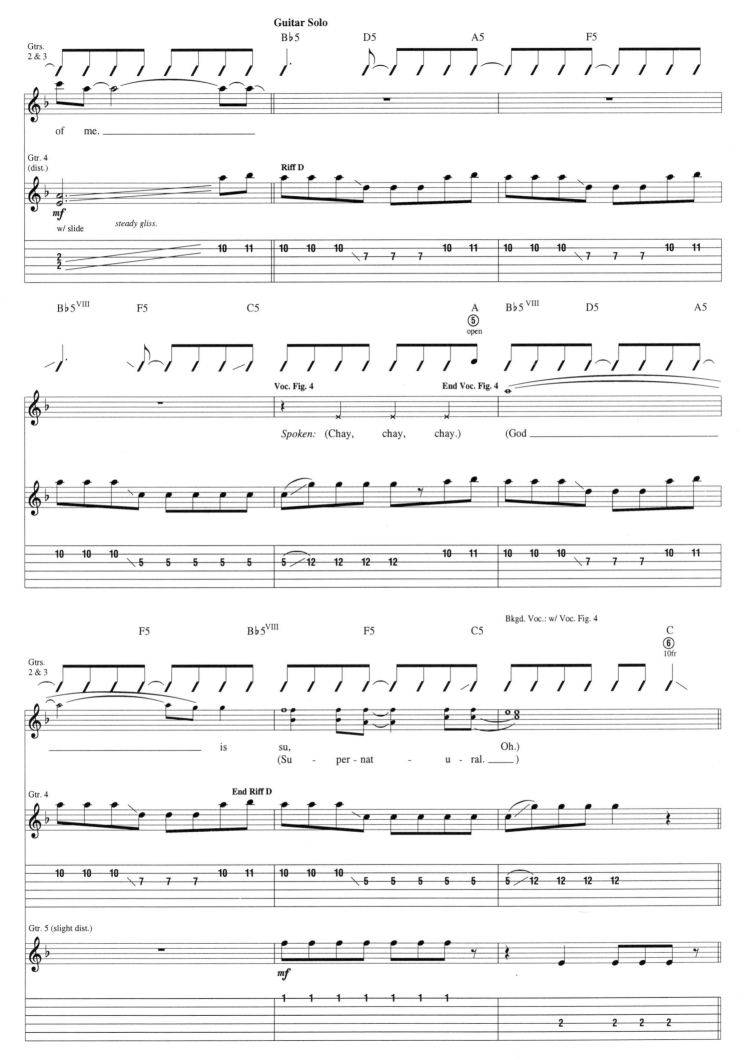

Chorus

Bkgd. Voc.: w/ Voc. Fig. 2
Gtrs. 2 & 3: w/ Rhy. Figs. 2 & 2A, 2 times, simile
Gtrs. 4 & 5 tacet

God is there _ and He ___ is watch-ing. The signs are ev - 'ry-where. _____ Oh, ___ God is there, _ there's no _

Spoken: (It's su-per-nat-u-ral.)

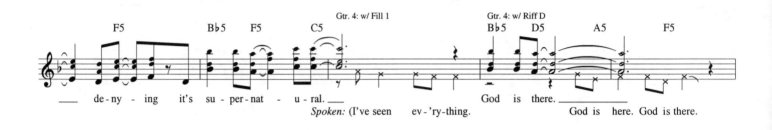

___ de-ny - ing it's su-per-nat - u-ral. ___ God is there. God is here. God is there.

Spoken: (I've seen ev - 'ry-thing.

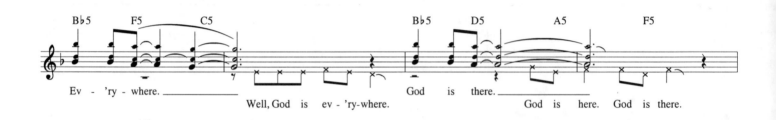

Ev - 'ry - where. _____ God is there. _____ God is here. God is there.

Well, God is ev - 'ry-where.

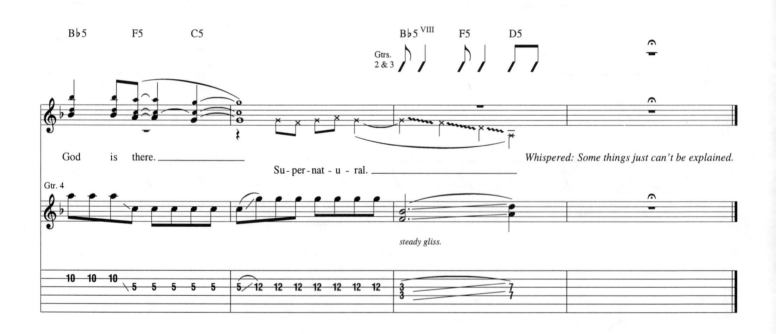

God is there. _____ Whispered: Some things just can't be explained.

Su - per-nat - u - ral. _____

steady gliss.

Red Letters

Words and Music by Toby McKeehan, Michael Tait, Kevin Max, Mark Heimermann and Chris Harris

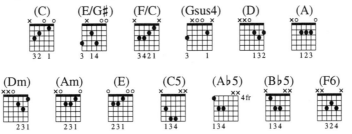

(C)   (E/G#)   (F/C)   (Gsus4)   (D)   (A)

(Dm)   (Am)   (E)   (C5)   (Ab5)   (Bb5)   (F6)

Gtr. 3; Tune Down 1/2 Step, Capo IV

Gtrs. 1, 2, 4 & 5 Tune Down 1/2 Step:

①=Eb ④=Db

②=Bb ⑤=Ab

③=Gb ⑥=Eb

Intro

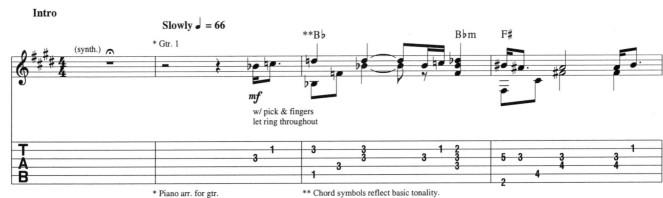

Slowly ♩ = 66

*Piano arr. for gtr.   **Chord symbols reflect basic tonality.

Verse

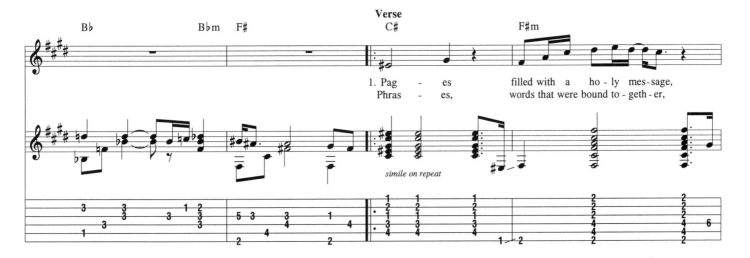

1. Pag - es   filled with a ho - ly mes - sage,
   Phras - es,   words that were bound to - geth - er,

sealed with a kiss from heav - en,   on a scroll, __ long   a - go. __
now have the power to sev - er,   like a sword, __ ev - er - more. __

* Symbols in parentheses represent chord names respective to capoed guitar and do not reflect actual sounding chord.

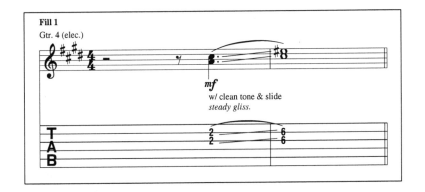

* Symbols in parentheses represent chord names respective to capoed guitar.
  Symbols above reflect actual sounding chord. Capoed fret is "0" in TAB.

** Gtr. 2 to left of slash in TAB.

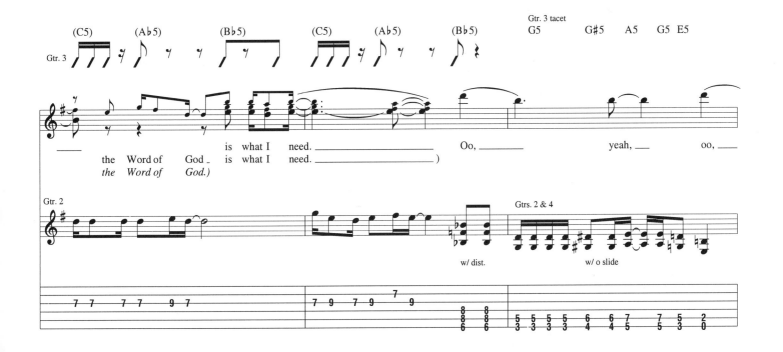

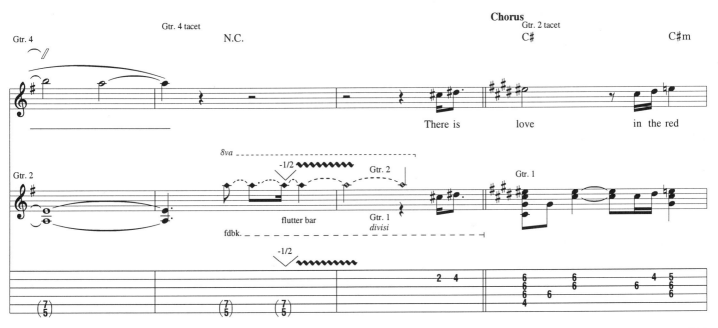